Colonel Unthank and the Gold

THE EXPANSION OF VICTORIAN NO

Clive Lloyd

Published in the United Kingdom by Clive Lloyd
colonelunthanksnorwich.com

Copyright © Clive Lloyd 2017
ISBN 978-1-5272-1576-4

All rights reserved. No portion of this book may be reproduced, stored in a retrieval system or transmitted at any time or by any means mechanical, electronic, photocopying, recording or otherwise, without the prior, written agreement of Clive Lloyd

Clive Lloyd has asserted his right to be identified as the author of this work in accordance with the Copyright, Designs and Patents act 1988.
The author has made every reasonable effort to provide correct historical data and to contact copyright holders of photographs. Please write to us for any inadvertent errors or omissions to be corrected in subsequent editions.

First printed 2017

Design by Karen Roseberry

CONTENTS

The Golden Triangle	6
The Unthanks	8
Who was Colonel Unthank?	16
Where did the Unthanks live in Heigham?	22
Houses named Heigham	25
The 'Unthank' wall	27
The break-up of the Unthank estate	30
The Heigham Lodge Estate	34
Heigham Grove Estate	35
Churches and chapels	38
The Eaton half of the Golden Triangle	42
Heigham Park	45
The Park Town Estate	48
The Avenue Estate	48
The southwestern Triangle	49
The Eaton Grove Estate	51
Newmarket Road	52
Acknowledgements	53
References	53

The development of Norwich's Golden Triangle is interwoven with the lives of three generations of the Unthank family. Others contributed land to the Triangle but the Unthank estate forms one of the largest blocks and it is their name that is commemorated in the thoroughfare – Unthank Road – that forms the backbone of this area of Victorian terraced housing (fig 1) [ref 1].

THE GOLDEN TRIANGLE

As long as residents and estate agents try to define a catchment area with good amenities on the university side of the city, the boundaries of the Golden Triangle will appear to be elastic. But I have always understood the Triangle to be that area of land between the inner ring road next to the city walls and the outer ring road a mile south (Mile End Road), bounded by Earlham Road and Newmarket Road with Unthank Road (dotted blue line) running down the middle of figure 1. The figure also demonstrates that this is certainly not a neat triangle unless you project its apex well into the city itself, beyond the inner ring road (dotted yellow line). However, the alternative – the Golden Trapezoid – doesn't have the same ring. Much of the non-Triangle land to the east of Newmarket Road, owned by the Town Close Estate, contains large plots occupied by generously-sized houses – even mansions – beyond the reach of the residents of the Triangle itself. On the west side of Earlham Road is another area of attractive Victorian terracing, based around St Philips and Sandringham Roads. In terms of the quality and style of housing this area shares much with the Triangle from which it seems unreasonably excluded, perhaps by distance from the parade of shops on Unthank Road or simply by the bother of shoe-horning it into an already distorted triangle.

Well into the nineteenth century Norwich city remained confined by its walls with little extramural development. The parish of Heigham, which abutted the southern wall, showed few signs of the expansion that was to follow: the

1. THE GOLDEN TRIANGLE
©1956 Ordnance Survey. Courtesy National Library of Scotland

1842 tithe map for Heigham [2] (part of which is now the Golden Triangle) still showed large areas of arable land with very few occupied houses (fig 2). By the time of the first Ordnance Survey of Norwich in the 1880s much of this open ground had disappeared under the street plan that essentially remains today. The 1842 tithe map was therefore made on the brink of the suburbanisation of Heigham.

2. 1842 TITHE MAP OF HEIGHAM.
Norfolk Record Office BR 276/1/0051. Open Government Licence.

3. PROPERTIES ASSOCIATED WITH THE UNTHANKS. UNTHANK ROAD IN YELLOW.
1842 Heigham tithe map. NRO BR 276/1/0051. Open Government Licence

4. THE WALL: THE LAST VESTIGE OF THE UNTHANK ESTATE?

In the late C18, William Unthank was among the first to move out beyond the city walls. There is some confusion surrounding the exact site of his house and on the 1842 tithe map I have marked three properties that relate to the uncertainty (fig 3). Thirty years ago I was told that an unusually tall stretch of wall at the junction of Clarendon and Unthank Roads was situated opposite the former site of Unthank's house and was the last vestige of the family estate (fig 4). Occasionally, I would hear this urban myth repeated as if it were fact and I became fascinated with it. By tracing the ownership of the wall the development of the Golden Triangle starts to unfold. But first, the Unthanks.

THE UNTHANKS

When I bought a house on the Unthank Road in the 1980s I was told that the name 'Unthank' referred to one thane's holding of land – a thane being a minor Early English aristocrat given land by the king in return for military service. An alternative interpretation is based on the Anglo-Saxon sense of negativity carried in the word 'unthank'. The linguist Peter Trudgill [3] suggests that certain Anglo-Saxon hamlets in the north of England were called unthanc-es, meaning that the inhabitants were living there without acknowledging that the hamlet belonged to someone else. The fact that this rare surname occurs most frequently on the formerly contested border between England and Scotland lends some credence to the idea. Indeed, most British villages named Unthank are concentrated in the north of England: Cumbria, Derbyshire, County Durham, Yorkshire and Northumberland.

William Unthank senior, who had come down to Norwich from Durham in the eighteenth century, was the son of Robert Unthank from the village of Unthank in Northumberland [4]. William senior is recorded in Rye's history of Heigham as being, "a pushing man of the Whiteley type" [5]. Although this simile has lost its meaning over more than 100 years we still get an impression that William was a go-getter. Between 1758 and 1790, he simultaneously ran several businesses in St Stephen's: corn merchant, salesman, and a barber who made perukes or periwigs towards the end of the fashion for such things. He also rented coaches and his house at No 2 Rampant Horse Street must have been conveniently close to the ancient Rampant Horse Inn, from which the London coaches departed.

William Unthank's son, William junior (1760-1837, Fig 6), trained to become a solicitor and in 1786 became partner to William Foster [6]. In 1798 Foster and Unthank's practice moved to Old Bank of England Court in Queen Street (Fosters is now one of the city's major law firms and is situated on Bank Plain). William Unthank – and from now on this will refer to William junior – was evidently an astute businessman like his father. Around 1833 he is said to have acquired much property from Reverend John Humfrey and his wife, thereby establishing the fortunes of his Norfolk descendants [5]. Reverend A.J. Nixseaman (vicar of Intwood, 1956-1967) mentions that William Unthank owned ca 2500 acres [7]. As well as land in the parishes of Eaton and

> The old Rampant Horse Inn was a large medieval timber-framed building with stabling for about 80 horses. The Curl brothers bought it in the C19 and demolished it to build their department store, Curls. This was bombed in the 1942 Baedeker Raids and replaced by the present-day Debenhams building. The mosaic of a black horse rearing on its hind legs, situated in Debenham's entrance opposite Marks and Spencer, is a reminder of its previous incarnation (Fig 5).

5. MOSAIC OUTSIDE DEBENHAMS, RAMPANT HORSE STREET

6. PORTRAIT OF WILLIAM UNTHANK Courtesy of Fosters Solicitors

Heigham – where this Unthank story is based – William Unthank had considerable country holdings at Bawburgh, Trowse and Lakenham, including 1,148 acres at Bedingham, 11 miles south of Norwich.

However, it was to the parish of Heigham, just outside St Giles' Gate, that he moved in 1793 from the parish of St Giles [7]. But before describing the encroachment of terraced housing across the Unthank estate we must get ahead of ourselves and learn something about the next two generations of Norwich Unthanks since the development of the Golden Triangle spanned their lifetimes rather than that of founding father, the second William Unthank.

In 1783, William Unthank married Ann May of Southwold and they raised a family of seven sons and two daughters. Records show that William erected a monument, in the Heigham parish church of St Bartholomew's (Fig 7), to Ann who died in 1820 age 57 [5]. The plaque – destroyed in the German air raids of 1942 – also recorded the premature loss of two of their sons: the eldest, William Samuel, who was killed in 1812 age 24 (at Badajoz, in Wellington's siege of a French garrison in Spain); and the sixth son, Robert, who died in 1820 age 21. It was in the same church that Clement William was to later install a plaque to the memory of his father (d. 1837 age 77) expressing his filial affection.

Clement William had good cause to record his indebtedness to his father for as the youngest son he had already received the lion's share of the Unthank estate, two years before William's death [7]. The second son, Thomas, received a legacy of £1000 and an annuity of £320 per annum. Sons 3 and 4 had emigrated to Australia and were not mentioned in the will. Son 5 was a lawyer and his provision was also not mentioned, nor was that of the two daughters. With the first and sixth sons dead, it was the seventh – Clement William – who received the bulk of his father's land. He would oversee the first phase of its sale and his experience as a lawyer in Foster and Unthank would help him draft the restrictive covenants that ensured the quality and character of the Unthank estate of terraced housing.

Clement William Unthank courted Mary Anne Muskett of Intwood Hall (Fig 8), a few miles south of Norwich. To visit her it is said that he rode his horse along a sandy back lane that became known as Unthank's Road [7]. They married in 1835, two years before Clement William's father died. We have yet to come to the vexed question of where exactly they lived in Norwich but we do know from an oil painting that their large house, somewhere in Heigham, was surrounded by pasture, grazed by cows [illustrated in ref 7]. They lived on this large estate until 1855 when Mary Anne inherited Intwood Hall following her own father's death. Mary Anne had four children: Mary Ann Clementine, Elizabeth Salusbury, Clement William Joseph (1847-1936) and John, who died in his last term at Eton College, aged 18.

When he was a captain in the 17th Lancers, Clement William Joseph Unthank (CWJ) married Judith Sarah, daughter of Onley Savill-Onley of Stisted Hall, Essex. In 1884, appreciating that his son CWJ would not have a generous

7. HEIGHAM ST BARTHOLOMEW.

army pension, Clement William made a living deed of gift in which he transferred all of his Heigham estate to his son, much as his own father had done 49 years earlier. So any development of the Unthank estate after 1884 occurred during CWJ's ownership.

Clement William was the first Unthank to live at Intwood Hall and when he died his widow Mary Ann began a campaign to get her son CWJ – who was living in Northamptonshire – to come back to Intwood. She built herself a dower house, the White House, but according to Reverend Nixseaman [7], her son refused to come back, claiming there was insufficient room at Intwood Hall for his growing family; he then had seven children, eventually ten. Mary Anne's promise to expand Intwood Hall, combined with a threat to give £10,000 to the Norwich and Norfolk Hospital if he didn't return, worked and CWJ took up residence in his boyhood home now transformed into a Gothic hall (Fig 8). CWJ devoted his life to hunting and it was in this guise as a country gentleman that he appears in portraits. He was photographed surrounded by hounds for in order to pursue hares and rabbits he had purchased the Dunston Harriers (fig 9). Later, when the dogs were kennelled at the dower house, they became known as the Intwood Harriers. Similarly, the 1896 oil painting by Lucien Besche (fig 10) illustrates him astride his horse with hounds Ringwood, Domino and Fencer at this feet. His devotion to country sport can be judged from the fact that until the First World War he would decamp to Lincolnshire for the hunting season.

8. INTWOOD HALL IN THE LATE C19 Courtesy Richard Gordon.

9. CWJ UNTHANK WITH THE INTWOOD HARRIERS. Courtesy Richard Gordon.

10. PORTRAIT OF CWJ UNTHANK BY LUCIEN BESCH Courtesy Julian Darling.

11. UNTHANK MEMORIAL WINDOW AT INTWOOD CHURCH.

Intwood Church, a field away from Intwood Hall, was where Clement William and Judith Sarah worshipped and it contains several memorials to them. The left panel of the rather beautiful Arts and Crafts window (fig 11) is dedicated to CWJ's father, Clement William, the right panel to his mother Mary Anne. Between them is the large central panel commemorating their son John, who died aged 21. CWJ and Judith Sarah (fig 12) dedicated the stained glass

13. LT CLEMENT WILLIAM ONLEY UNTHANK Courtesy of Richard Gordon

window in the south chancel to their daughter Judith Marion who also died at a young age, 23. Several tiles and brass plaques mark the passing of other family members but particularly poignant is the plaque in Victorian Gothic lettering to Lt. Clement William Onley Unthank who died at Lucknow, India, in 1900 (fig 13). The memorial erected by his fellow soldiers records that he died, "From the effects of a fall at polo" (fig 14). Onley Street in the Golden Triangle, near the Unthank's Heigham House, was also named in his memory.

12. PORTRAIT OF JUDITH SARAH UNTHANK
Courtesy Richard Gordon.

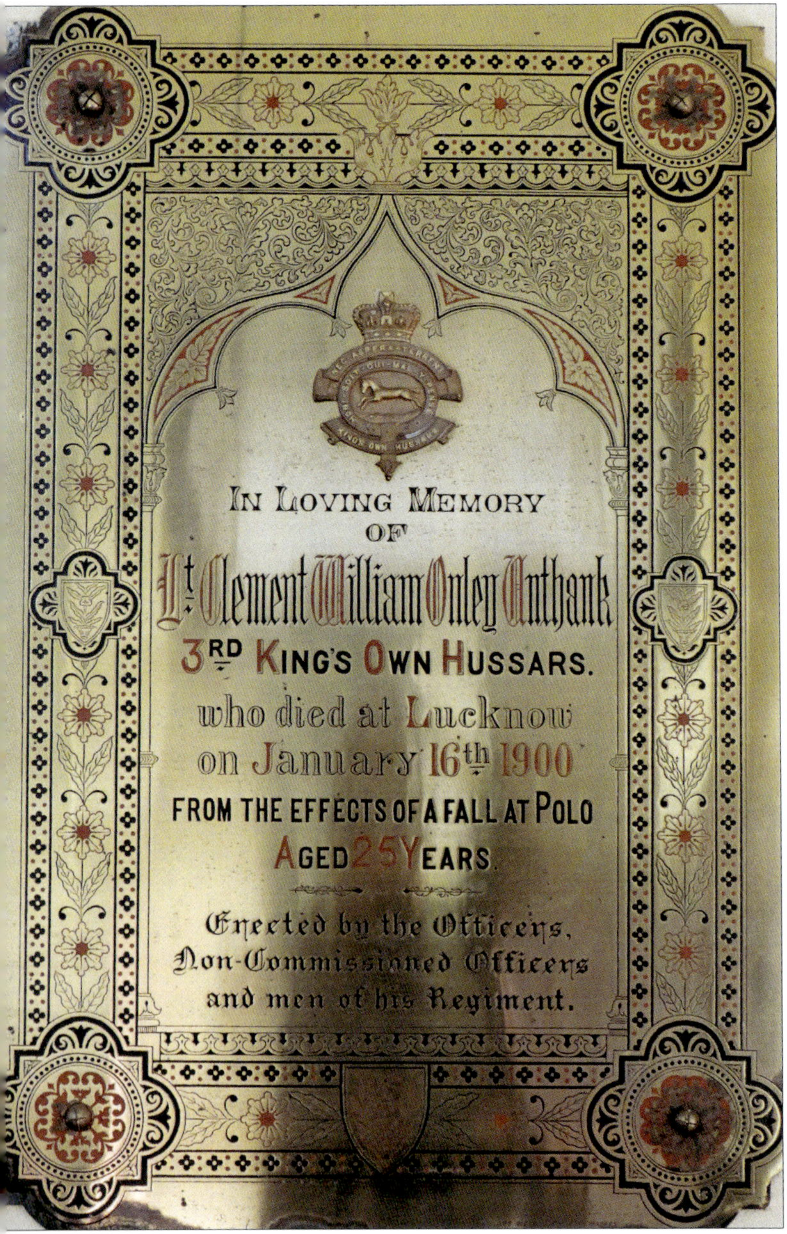

WHO WAS COLONEL UNTHANK?

Not one but three members of the Unthank family were entitled to be known as Colonel Unthank. The first was Clement William (1804-1884) who, as Deputy Lieutenant of Norfolk, was involved in raising volunteers for the Crimean War. His son CWJ Unthank (1847-1936) was a captain in the 17th Lancers and in later life was known as the Old Colonel - he also served with the Norfolk Volunteers. Figures 15 and 16 show CWJ with two sons, of whom John would be the last Colonel Unthank. Colonel John Salusbury Unthank DSO, MC (1875-1959) fought in both the Boer and the First World War. Perhaps his enrolment in the Durham Light Infantry represented a nod towards the family's origins in the North-East. When Reverend AJ Nixseaman wrote his Story of Intwood in the 1970s [7], there were people who still remembered this third Colonel Unthank (d. 1959). Nixseaman tells the tale of the bluff old soldier taking his seat at the front of Intwood Church. We obtain a sense of his position in the community from the fact that when he stood up to take off his mackintosh the congregation behind him stood up as well.

14. MEMORIAL PLAQUE TO CWO UNTHANK, INTWOOD CHURCH

15. JOHN SALUSBURY, CWJ AND CLEMENT WILLIAM ONLEY UNTHANK AT 'FRITTON' Courtesy Richard Gordon.

16. PARENTS JUDITH SARAH AND CWJ UNTHANK WITH JUDITH, JOHN, CLEM AND JANET Courtesy Richard Gordon.

Bat. Norfolk Volunteers

17. COLONEL CWJ UNTHANK, SEATED 4TH LEFT, WITH THE NORFOLK VOLUNTEERS *Courtesy Richard Gordon*

18. MEMORIAL PLAQUE TO JOHN SALUSBURY UNTHANK

19. CWJ UNTHANK SITTING WITH HIS FAVOURITE GUN DOG VICTOR Courtesy Richard Gordon

20. OFFICERS OF THE KING'S OWN HUSSARS 1896. CWO SEATED FAR LEFT Courtesy Richard Gordon.

21. CWO UNTHANK

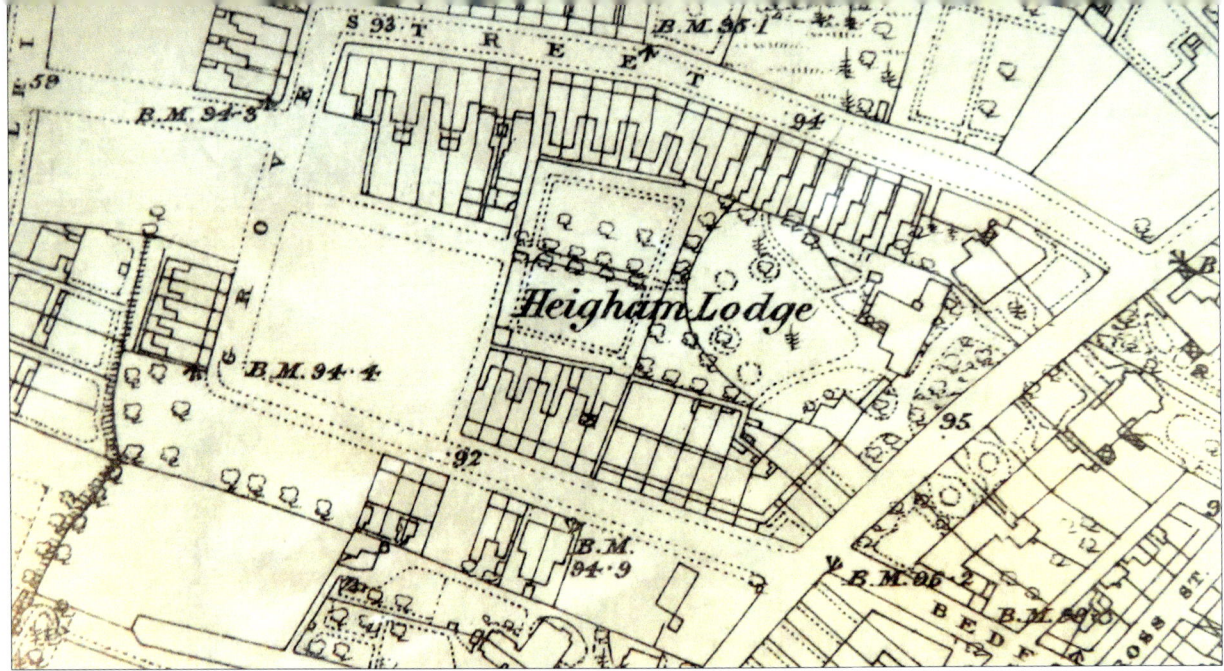

22. HEIGHAM HOUSE/LODGE, JUNCTION OF PRESENT-DAY CLARENDON AND UNTHANK ROADS.
© Ordnance Survey 1883. Norfolk Heritage Centre

WHERE DID THE UNTHANKS LIVE IN HEIGHAM?

Reverend Nixseaman's book about Intwood is the major source of information about the Norwich Unthanks [7]. As we have just seen, Intwood was to play a significant part in the Unthank story for Clement William's move to Intwood Hall in 1855 was to free his Heigham estate for house-building. Nixseaman states that William Unthank and his successors had lived at Heigham House for around a hundred years (1793-1891), "at Heigham House in a lovely parkland setting, outside the city walls not far from St Giles' Gates … newly built with 70 acres of grass and woods". St Giles' Gates once stood at the top of Upper St Giles Street and any remnants are now under the ring road on Grapes Hill. The romantic description of this parkland setting seems to have been prompted by a painting then in the possession of William Unthank's last direct descendant, his great great granddaughter Margaret Beatrice (d.1995), the owner of the Manor of Intwood.

According to the six-inch version of the Ordnance Survey map published in 1887 the property between present-day Clarendon and Grosvenor Roads is Heigham House, while the 1883 1:2500 OS map labelled the exact same property 'Heigham Lodge' (fig 22). Either way, house or lodge, this location is undoubtedly the one referred to by Reverend Nixseaman [7]. We know this because he also wrote that Heigham House was demolished in 1891 and that the site was then occupied by Cavell House, the Innisfallen Hotel and other buildings. A search through Kelly's Norwich Directory for 1960 shows that this hotel was at 32/34 Unthank Road while Cavell House at 36 provided a home nursing service. Both addresses are near the junction of Clarendon and Unthank Roads and this level of detail provides a specific location for the Unthanks' home. To drive the point home Reverend Nixseaman stated that all that now remained of the Unthanks' mansion was a piece of walling, which had formed part of the stables, "at the corner of Ampthill Street, opposite Clarendon Road." This piece of local folklore therefore seems to have originated with Reverend Nixseaman.

But beware the rosy glow of hindsight for not all of the details in Reverend Nixseaman's account ring true. Ampthill Street is not opposite Clarendon Road and Clement William and his family did not live in this house from the time they married (1835) until they moved to Intwood Hall (1855). The 1842 tithe map shows that a house and substantial landholdings belonging to Clement William Unthank were based quite some distance away around present-day Onley Street. The 1851 census records that CW and his wife were living there with a household comprised of two daughters, two sons and eight servants. And from 1836 – one year before William Unthank's death – Timothy Steward of Steward and Patteson's Brewery can be shown to have been living in Heigham House at the corner of Clarendon Road. Importantly, the poll records show that Steward lived in the parish as an owner/occupier: that is, his house was his own and therefore not rented from the Unthank family.

Further evidence that the Unthanks lived further along Unthank Road, and nowhere near The Wall, is provided by Morant's map of 1873 (fig 23), which shows an estate labelled 'The Unthanks' in the area of present-day Onley Street. It was still there in the first Ordnance Survey of Norwich (1879-1886). These dates are too late for William Unthank, who died in 1837, but the Norfolk Record Office holds a map for a triangular piece of garden ground on the west side of the road [8]. On the east side there is a corner of a plot labelled as the property of 'Wm Unthank

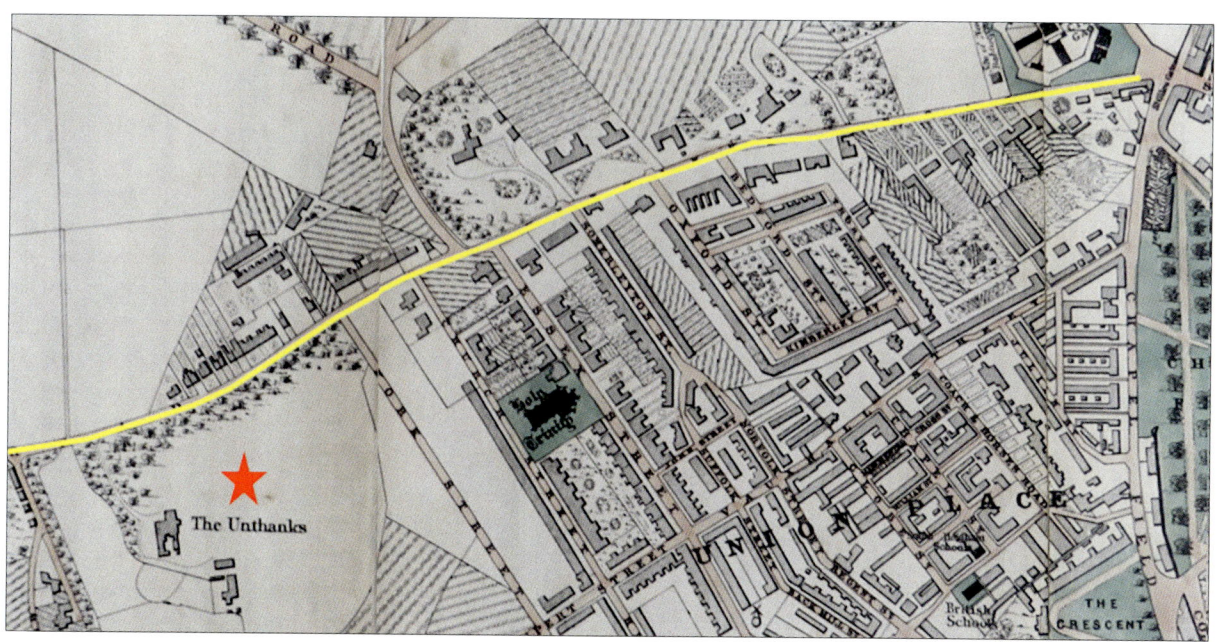

23. AW MORANT'S MAP, NORWICH 1873. 'THE UNTHANKS' (RED STAR) NEAR PRESENT-DAY ONLEY STREET OFF 'UNTHANKS' ROAD (YELLOW LINE). Courtesy Norfolk Heritage Centre

Esq' and is consistent with the Onley Street location. There are, therefore, several pieces of evidence to say that the Unthanks' estate was based around present-day Onley Street while there is no independent corroboration of Nixseaman's hypothesis about the Clarendon Road site nearer the city.

Over the years, correspondents to the local press have also queried the site of Unthank's House. A letter in the Norfolk Advertiser, dated 30th June 1983, was from an Unthank – Margaret Beatrice of Intwood Hall, the great, great granddaughter of William Unthank:

'The wall on the left of your picture is, I am told, all that remains of the stables of Heigham House, which was demolished in 1891. I enclose for your information a photograph of a picture I have of the house and park." M. Unthank, Intwood Hall.

The picture of "the wall on the left" was of the low (one metre high) garden walls still to be seen along a small terrace of Boardman-designed houses at the city end of Unthank Road, not the unusually tall 'stable' wall that Nixseaman had identified in his book. The other "photograph of a picture … of the house and park" to which Miss Unthank refers is identical to the one that Nixseaman used in his book suggesting that it was he who directed her ("I am told") to the Clarendon Road site.

However, the newspaper debate about the Unthanks' house goes back long before that. In 1934 a correspondent, initialled WB, wrote to the Eastern Daily Press:

"In reply to S.B. about 60 years ago Colonel Unthank's House was near Mount Pleasant and, if my memory is correct, was in the space now occupied by Gloucester, Bury and Onley Streets. His grounds were enclosed by a brick wall and the house was some distance from the road. The Unthank Arms, at the top of Newmarket Street, at one time bore, as a sign, the elaborate armorial bearings of the Unthanks, so we may, I think, assume with some confidence that the family existed in the neighbourhood". Eastern Daily Press May 25 1934.

This takes us back to within living memory of Unthank House and, indeed, in the same round of correspondence there is a letter from Colonel Unthank himself, Clement William Joseph (b 1847) [4]. The tone of the full quotation reveals a determination to set things straight:

"There are two letters in the EDP to-day referring to the Unthank Road, which was so-called after my grandfather, who was born in 1760 and was a partner in a firm of solicitors, of whom Sir Wm Foster was the senior member. My grandfather bought Heigham House and 70 acres of land between what is now Trinity Street and Mount Pleasant about 1793, and my father, born in 1804, was a partner in the firm until 1855, when we came to live here at Intwood Hall, which belonged to my mother. Heigham House was pulled down about forty years ago and the only buildings in the parish with which we can claim any connexion now are Trinity church built on a site given by my father, and the Bishop Pelham Memorial Chapel [Bishop of Norwich d.1894] on a site given by me. My grandfather was the great grandson of Robert Unthank of Unthank in Northumberland; so we cannot claim any connexion with Norwich earlier than my grandfather. Yours faithfully, CWJ Unthank, Intwood Hall". Eastern Daily Press May 25 1934.

Coming from someone who lived in the Onley Street house until he was eight, when his family moved to Intwood Hall, this definitively skewers Reverend Nixseaman's rosy view of an estate within sight of St Giles' Gate. This location is also consistent with Walter Rye's History of the Parish of Heigham (1917) in which he wrote that Unthank's house was on the other side of the road to Timothy Steward's house [5]. Rye also described the house as being in well-wooded grounds, which chimes with the depiction of Unthank's House in the 1842 tithe map.

Significantly, in his letter to the Eastern Daily Press, CWJ Unthank referred to his former home as Heigham House [4]. As we shall see, in the second part of the nineteenth century several other large houses included the name Heigham, which may explain why, a full century after the Unthanks departed for Intwood, Reverend Nixseaman simply selected the wrong Heigham House on which to anchor his story of the family.

HOUSES NAMED HEIGHAM

We have already seen that Timothy Steward's Heigham House was also named Heigham Lodge on some maps. But – in addition to Heigham House near present-day Onley Street, of which Reverend Nixseaman seemed oblivious – at least three others can be added to the mix. Outside the Golden Triangle, but still in Heigham, was the medieval Heigham Hall at the junction between Heigham Street and Old Palace Road. A butcher named John Lowden, who made his fortune as a contractor in the Napoleonic Wars, bought the hall in the early C19 and partly renovated it [5]. Its ironic local name of Marrowbone House appears on Bryant's map of 1826 (fig 24) but C20 correspondence [9] indicates it was also known as Heigham House. Ten years later it was bought by two local doctors who opened it as a 'Private Lunatic Asylum' [10].

This latter Heigham House became relevant to the development of the Golden Triangle when another 'private madhouse' – Heigham Retreat – opened not far from Park Lane. The 1842 tithe map [2] shows that the carriage drive to this property branched off Park Lane – sometimes called Asylum Lane – near the junction with Mill Hill Road (fig 25). The map illustrates that the large building was approached up a tree-lined avenue, the first part of which overlaps present-day Avenue Road. Three doctors had bought the property from Mr Jollye of Loddon and it was during their tenure that, in 1852, The Retreat became embroiled in scandal [11]. Reverend Edmund Holmes was witnessed attempting to violate a young girl and it would appear that a local magistrate helped this member 'of a good county family' from being convicted of rape by declaring him

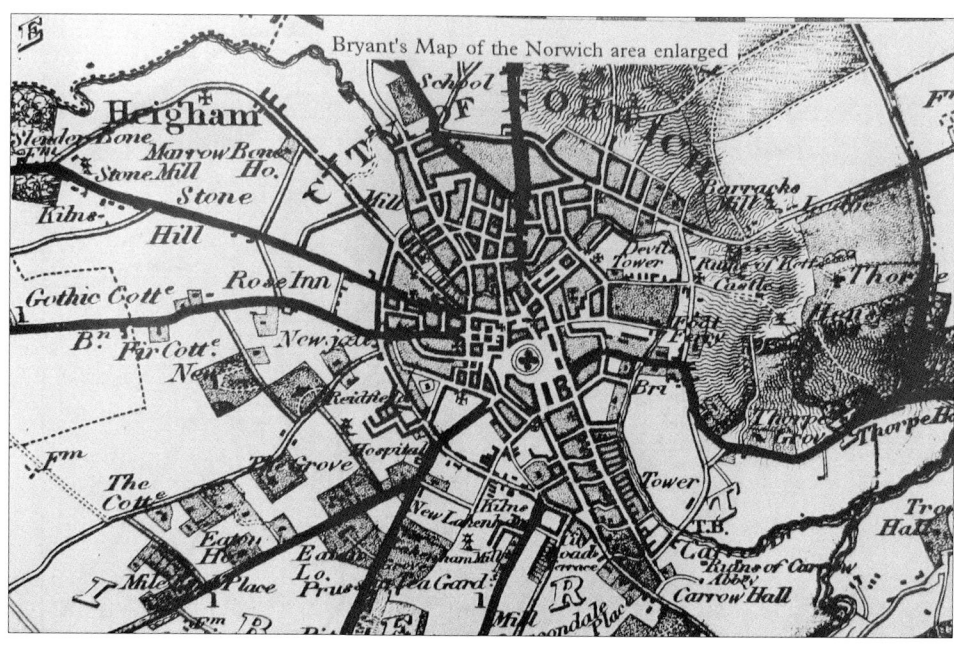

24. MARROWBONE HOUSE (BENEATH 'HEIGHAM' TOP LEFT). BRYANT'S MAP, NORWICH 1826.
Courtesy Norfolk Heritage Centre

insane. Holmes was admitted to The Retreat where his insanity proved to be no hindrance to his appointment as its chaplain. Contemporary notes convey the deep sense of local outrage at this gross injustice but the case did at least lead to a change in the law.

In 1859 Heigham Retreat (fig 26) was bought by its competitor, Heigham (Marrowbone) Hall, who promptly closed it down but its outline is commemorated in the layout of the Welsh-named terraces that followed. The site of The Retreat itself lies between Swansea Road and the top (east) end of Caernarvon Road. Pembroke and Denbigh Roads adhere closely to two of the estate's boundaries while Cardiff Road bisects the estate, connecting Avenue Road to Denbigh Road.

Another Heigham House on the fringes of the Golden Triangle occupied a one-acre plot at the corner of Heigham Road and West Pottergate Street; it was adjacent to St Philip's church, which was demolished in 1977. Dressed stone and a font from the church can still be seen in the grounds of the care home that now occupies the site.

25. THE RETREAT (GREEN STAR) ON 1842 HEIGHAM TITHE MAP. PARK LANE, YELLOW. Open Government Licence

26. HEIGHAM RETREAT, ENGRAVING BY HENRY NINHAM. NRO MC279/6

THE 'UNTHANK' WALL

If the Unthanks' Heigham estate was centred around present-day Onley Street, who did own the stretch of unusually tall wall (fig 4) opposite the Clarendon/Unthank Road junction? White's Gazetteer of Norwich for 1836 lists Timothy Steward ('Brewer', of the Norwich brewery of Steward and Patteson) as being the owner of Heigham House/Lodge and an undated map in the NRO explicitly labels this 'Steward's House'.[12] In 1877 Edward Boardman surveyed the site and broke it down into plots for sale (fig 27); we should note that the sale did not include the land protected by 'The Wall' on the other side of the road [ref 13].

The initials of Steward and Patteson, S&P, can be seen on the keystone above a window on the Eaton Cottage public house, which is at the northern boundary of Eaton parish (fig 28).

That high wall protecting the back of the property on the opposite (east) side of Unthank Road did not, however, belong to Steward or even – as has been suggested – provide distant stabling for CW Unthank on his 'Onley Street' estate. Instead, the apportionment record accompanying the 1842 tithe map reveals that the property opposite belonged to the Trustees of Norwich Boys' Hospital. This charity, founded in 1617 by mayor Thomas Anguish, leased land in and around the city in order to maintain a boys' and a girls' hospital. Account ledgers held at the Norfolk Record Office [14] confirm that the charity's only land in Heigham was this long, narrow strip on the east side of Unthank Road, known as Peddars Acre (fig 29).

The entry for 1834 reads, "Of Richard Harmer for a messuage [buildings] & land without St Giles Gates let to him from Michaelmas 1822 for 60 years £15-0-0." The ledger for 1837 states that Harmer leased both house and garden. The 1842 tithe map records that Leonard Harmer (son?) leased the land from the Trustees of the Boys'

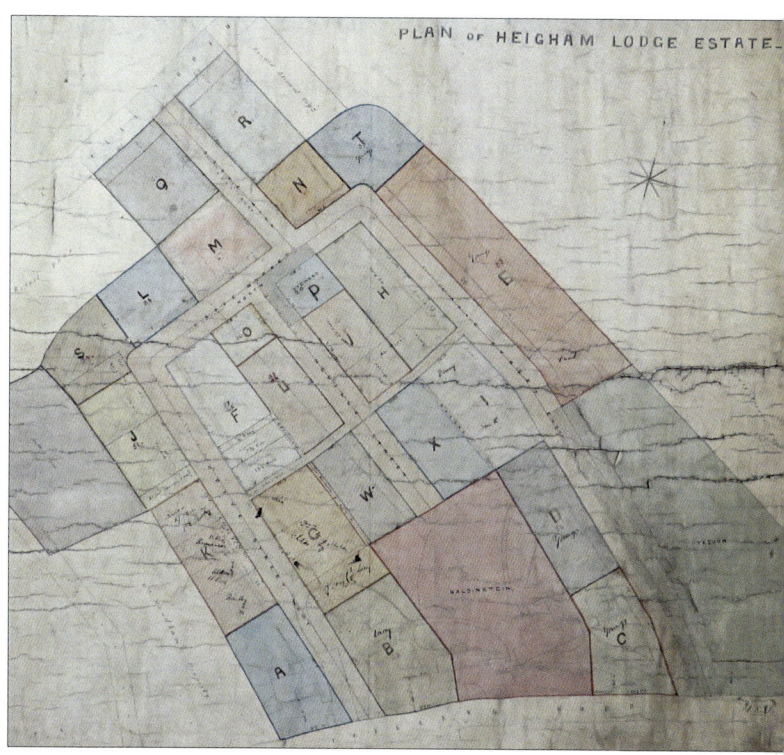

27. PLAN OF EATON LODGE ESTATE, EDWARD BOARDMAN 1877.
NRO MC 191/2

28. STEWARD AND PATTESON KEYSTONE ON EATON COTTAGE PUBLIC HOUSE.

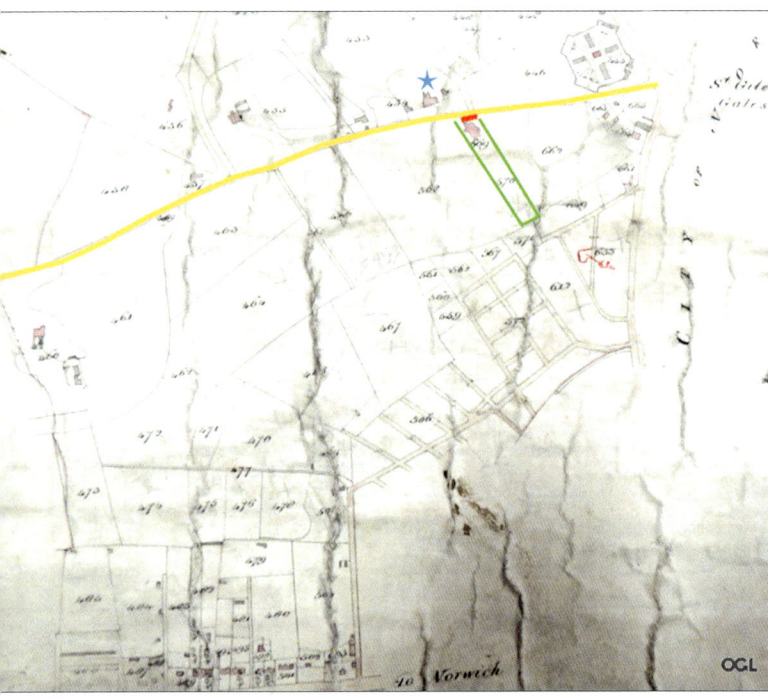

29. PEDDARS ACRE (GREEN) OPPOSITE STEWARD'S HOUSE (BLUE STAR). 1842 HEIGHAM TITHE MAP.
NRO BR 276/1/0051. Open Government Licence.

Hospital as well as owning two hemmed-in plots to the rear. The hospital's ledgers show that amongst the names of others who took on the lease until at least 1897, the names of Unthank and Steward are absent. One significant name that does appear over the period 1854-1865 is that of an inn-keeper William Trory, who is commemorated in Trory Street. We will come to this shortly.

The key point is that from 1822 (i.e., 15 years before William Unthank's death) to well beyond Clement William's departure to Intwood Hall and the ensuing break-up of the Unthank estate, The Wall opposite Steward's House did not belong to the Unthank family. We must therefore say farewell to the urban myth that the tall wall was part of the Unthanks' stables.

In a little while we will come to the break-up of Steward's estate on both sides of the Unthank Road but in the meantime it is worth noting that the restrictive covenants attached to the sale of land provide a possible explanation for the unusual height of The Wall. Timothy Steward sold land opposite his house (i.e., the east side of Unthank Road) to William Trory who, in 1853, re-sold the land for development [15]. To protect privacy on his own garden ground Trory inserted a covenant into the sale agreement requiring the purchasers to build around their property a substantial six-foot wall with 14-inch piers capped with coping bricks. As a further safeguard against being overlooked, no facing windows or apertures were to be inserted into the new houses. But an even more stringent restriction had been inserted by Steward in the original agreement. He insisted that before any land could be developed an entire dwelling house facing Unthank Road had to be built between his house and any 'offices' (i.e., lavatories) at the rear of any subsequently built houses (fig 30). Stricter still, no such nuisance was to be visible from Timothy and Lucy Steward's 'first floor or first story' (sic) – literally a tall order. This strongly points to the double-height wall at the front of Peddars Acre being built to prevent any unpleasantness being seen by the Stewards as they peeped out of their bedroom windows.

An interesting tailpiece on The Wall can be found in the ledgers of the Trustees of the Boys' Hospital [14]. In 1883 the name of the lessee of Peddars Acre (at this time CF Hinde) was joined by that of JB Parker under 'Right of Way'. This provides an explanation for the narrow doorway in The Wall: allowing Mr Parker access between Unthank Road and the otherwise hemmed-in land to the rear (fig 31).

30. OPPOSITE STEWARD'S HOUSE ON UNTHANK ROAD.

31. ACCESS DOOR IN THE WALL.

THE BREAK-UP OF THE UNTHANK ESTATE

When, in 1835, Clement William agreed to marry Mary Anne Muskett of Intwood Hall the marriage settlement indicates that he entered his Heigham estate in trust. In addition to over 23 acres that he occupied himself, he leased out three other blocks in Heigham amounting to just over 28 acres, totalling 52 acres in all. The manor court books – in which all land transactions were entered – gave a slightly different figure for the Unthank estate [16]. Two years before father William died, the records reveal that "in consideration of the natural love and affection" he transferred to his youngest son, Clement William Unthank, six acres in Eaton together with 68 acres 2 roods and 30 perches of land in Heigham.

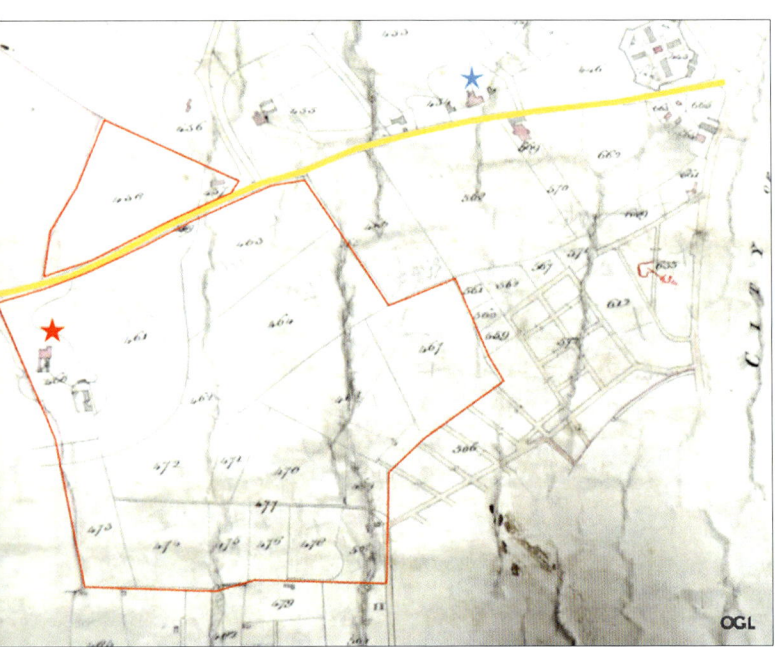

32. CW UNTHANK'S TITHABLE PLOTS IN HEIGHAM (RED). UNTHANK ROAD (YELLOW). 1842 TITHE MAP.
NRO BR 276/1/0051. Open Government Licence.

In 1837 William Unthank died at his son-in-law's house in Eaton after "severe suffering for several years, in patient resignation to his affliction" [17]. William was interred in the Heigham parish church of St Bartholomew's but, with the exception of the two sons who died in their twenties, the succeeding generations of Norfolk Unthanks were to be buried at Intwood church.

Five years after the transfer of Unthank land to Clement William, his own house and grounds in Heigham comprised a handful of tithable plots while he leased about 16 more. But in 1843, now living at Intwood Hall, he was asking the Heigham commissioners for his land rent charges (in lieu of church tithes) to be reduced "since the lands have been divided into numerous building plots" [18]. Further requests concerning rent charges were made in 1850 for another 46 acres and in 1878 for a further 10 [18]. As figure 32 illustrates, this covers a block of land mainly on the east side of Unthank Road stretching from present day Onley Street to north of Trinity Street. This estate was developed in stages [19]. From 1849 to 1883 land sale agreements held at the Norfolk Record Office show plots sold off in small blocks throughout this period: for example, for four houses in Cambridge Street [20]. Sale No 1 commenced in 1849, the second in 1852. The third sale included land between Essex and Trinity Streets where Holy Trinity Church was built in 1861 to accommodate the influx of worshippers into the parish. In that year the population of Heigham stood at 13,894 while 60 years earlier – just after William Unthank moved out of the city – it had been 854.

Most of the plots were sold to people associated with the building trade. Dozens of purchasers could have led to a conglomeration of styles but what gives the area its unity was the quality of the restrictive covenants imposed by CW Unthank [19]. Big houses for the middle classes tended to be built on more expensive plots towards Unthank Road while

33. GAUGED-BRICK DOORWAY ARCH ON THE FORMER KIMBERLEY ARMS.

further back along the side streets, smaller houses were built for the artisan class on less costly parcels of land. But, big or small, all had to obey a long list of strict requirements that affected the appearance of the estate as a whole.

As a solicitor well-practiced in drafting contracts Clement William was able to ensure that others would continue to adhere to his vision. For instance, houses were to be faced in good white bricks. Suffolk Whites from Somerleyton were used as well as Cossey Whites from Guntons' Brickyard at nearby Costessey. In the days of horse-drawn transport, local materials were inevitably favoured but the arrival of the railways in the mid C19 meant that other materials could be brought in from further afield. The Unthank covenants specified the use of slates and these could now be delivered from North Wales. Tiles made from local clay could be used for roofing but only if they met the approval of Clement William Unthank or his heirs.

Another requirement was that all doorways were to be arched (fig 33). This involved the use of gauged bricks – bricks moulded in concentric templates – that are characteristic of the Norwich terraced house [21]. This might have had something to do with the paucity of stone (for lintels) in Norfolk. Manufactured in an arched template the door arch could be easily reconstructed on site; the downward thrust of the building above locked the bricks into place so that the arch did not require such thick layers of mortar. In his authoritative book The English Terraced House [21], Stefan Muthesius noted that white brick was typical for Norwich with red bricks and red clay pantiles relegated to the rear ('Queen Anne in front, Sally Ann behind'). In a sea of white clay bricks the presence of red gauged bricks alternating with white on the door arches on some houses in Newmarket Street, and some red-brick door arches in Cambridge Street, therefore comes as a surprise. Nevertheless, stylistic variations on the Unthank estate tended to be minor.

Every building was to have iron gutters. Every building should have only sash windows, except shops. No building was to be more than two storeys high. Other restrictions prohibited the addition of gable peaks to the front of the house and no porch or projection was allowed to extend more than 18 inches from the building line unless agreed by CW Unthank. As a result the regular height and flatness of the terrace (fig 34) conveys a much diluted impression of the grander Palladian terraces seen, for instance, in Bath

34. TRINITY STREET, AN EARLY UNTHANK TERRACE.

35. THE UNTHANK ARMS ON NEWMARKET STREET.

and Edinburgh. Norfolk – based on deep layers of chalk interspersed with flint – is almost devoid of good building stone; as a consequence, architect William Kent had to use expensive white bricks for Holkham Hall on the north Norfolk coast [20]. John 'Bank of England' Soane had also resorted to white bricks for the building of Shotesham Hall [21]; this was only a short ride from Intwood Hall and would have been well known to Clement William.

The regular, white-brick terraces in Heigham may not so much ape the houses of the upper classes as represent a genuine attempt to apply high principles to urban planning at a time when large numbers of citizens within the city walls were living in crowded and insanitary courtyards. Perhaps a salutary lesson had been learned from an earlier C19th expansion outside the city walls. Crooks Place and Union Place were part of the New City, built between 1815 and 1835 just south of Chapelfield Gardens. Morant's map (fig 23) shows that these areas from the late Georgian era were situated either side of The Crescent. However, this New City was no shining example: its highly insanitary houses were demolished as slums after World War II but the fine Crescent remains. The subsequent Victorian development of South Heigham, where the great majority of housing survives, succeeded because of enlightened bye-laws and building acts that were passed in the second half of the 19th century [19].

On the Unthank estate, no building was to be used as a public house, or house for the sale of beer, ale, porter or spirituous liquors. One consequence of this was that large public houses did not punctuate the terraces but were positioned on individual corner sites, as occupied by the York Tavern, the Rose Tavern and – not far from Unthank's House – The Unthank Arms (now The Unthank (fig 35). The Unthank and The York Tavern on Unthank territory share a very similar design with The Garden House at the corner of Denbigh and Pembroke Roads on the other side of Unthank Road: all three have the main door on the chamfered corner and two large rounded windows either side.

The map by the City Surveyor, AW Morant (fig 23), shows that by 1873 the first release of Unthank land had resulted in the building of terraced housing on Essex Street; Holy Trinity Church had also been built between Essex Street and Church Street (as Trinity Street was initially called). A few years later the first Ordnance Survey of Norwich (1879-1886) reveals patchy development of Cambridge and York Streets. Progress to the plan we know today was blocked by the presence of 'Unthanks House' – as it was still labelled on the map – because the house and grounds remained in private hands. As a consequence, Rupert, Leicester and Newmarket Streets, which ran roughly parallel to Unthank Road, had not yet reached their full southward extent and were still to connect with roads that would be built across the grounds of the former Unthank home.

Walter Rye, in his History of the Parish of Heigham [5], states that Sir Charles Gilman lived in Unthanks House after the Unthanks departed. This would be Charles Rackham Gilman who later moved to Stafford House in Newmarket Road, now part of Norwich High School for Girls. Gilman was twice mayor but is better known for establishing the Norwich and London Accident Insurance Association that was acquired in 1909 by Norwich Union [22].

According to Rosemary O'Donoghue in her book on the expansion of Norwich [18], Clement William Joseph continued to sell off land into the C20 and this would have included his minor six-acre holding in the parish of Eaton – a triangle of land on the west side of Unthank Road. Restrictive covenants relating to houses built on Dover Street were unchanged from those imposed by his father. O'Donoghue remarks that the preponderance of small terraces without a hall entrance on Dover Street compares unfavourably with the quality of housing on Essex, Cambridge and Trinity Streets, which were built in the time of his father, Clement William. Certainly, in terms of appearance the early terraces were fairly plain but as new rows of houses advanced upon Unthank's House on present-day Onley Street the previously characteristic gauged-brick arches gave way to cheaper lintels made of reconstituted stone, and a greater incidence of protruding bay windows.

THE HEIGHAM LODGE ESTATE

Almost 20 years after Clement William moved to Intwood Hall, progress was slow in developing the Unthank's Heigham estate. By contrast, the development of Timothy Steward's Heigham Lodge Estate just to the north was already well advanced. Opposite his house on Unthank Road was a large plot of land that is labelled on the 1842 tithe map as Steward's Home Close (fig 36). In 1852 Steward sold some of this land to William Trory who, one year later sold it on to John Freeman, a builder, and Richard Bexfield, a boot and shoemaker (and presumably the speculator providing finance)[15].

Steward also sold some of Home Close, on the east side of Unthank Road, to William Griffin and Daniel Balls[15]. The sale documents are interesting – not just for the restrictive covenants relating to high walls and privacy – but for covenants that were similar to those used by the Unthank estate to ensure building quality. For example, the house was to be built "of good sound and white bricks, or of white stucco"; only sash windows were to be used etc. The Kimberley Arms was to be built on the corner of this block and cleaning of the brickwork in 2016-2017 drew attention to the quality of the white gauged bricks around the doorway, matching that seen on the Unthank estate (fig 33).

We can get a sense of Steward's holdings from the 1842 tithe map (fig 36). Opposite the large area of land around his own house on the west side of Unthank Road were two large plots running approximately from Trory Street to Somerleyton Street. One was Home Close and the other, which extended along the eastern edge of Unthank Road down to a boundary with the Unthank estate, he leased from the Trustees of the Boys' Hospital. On Home Close a small gridwork of streets was built, comprised of Trory and Oxford Streets running at right angles to Unthank Road with Ampthill Street coming between them. Running parallel to Unthank Road were Kimberley and Woburn Streets. However, Steward's insistence that a building facing Unthank Road had to be inserted between his house and this new development (fig 30) meant that Trory Street was denied an exit onto Unthank Road. Originally, Ampthill Street did open onto Unthank Road but in the last quarter of the C20 it was pedestrianised and made a cul-de-sac so that only Oxford Street now provides the estate's access onto Unthank Road.

Steward's own house and grounds on the west side of Unthank Road were also sold for development. According to the 1877 map drawn up by local surveyor and architect, Edward Boardman, the Eaton Lodge Estate was now

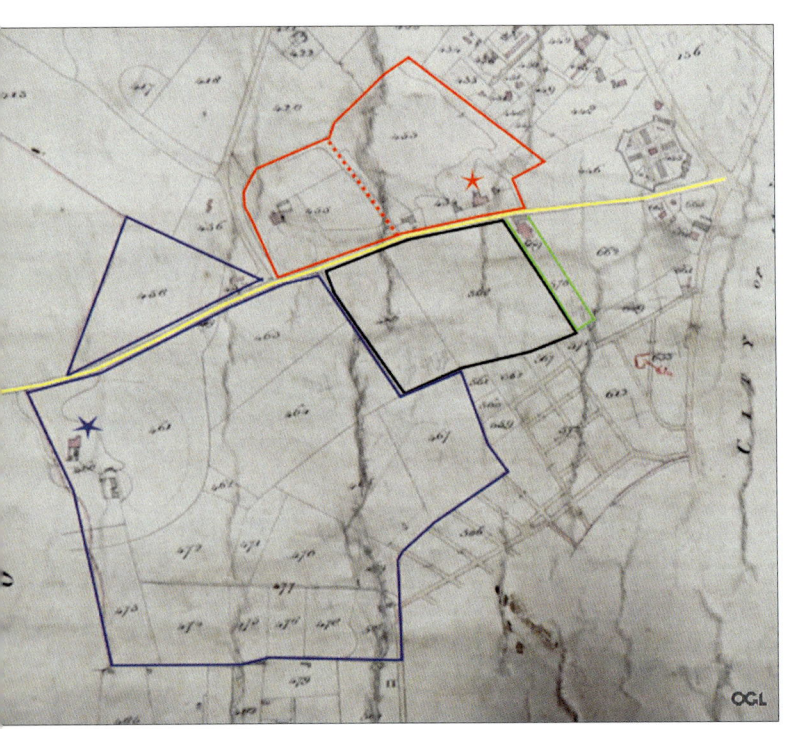

36. TIMOTHY STEWARD'S ESTATE (RED); PEDDARS ACRE (GREEN); STEWARD'S HOME CLOSE PLUS LAND RENTED FROM THE BOYS' HOSPITAL (BLACK); UNTHANK'S ESTATE (BLUE). 1842 Heigham tithe map. Open Government Licence.

subdivided into 20 blocks (fig 27.[23]). The owners included well-known builders like Lacey and the firm of Youngs (now part of RG Carter). At one time the estate fronted a stretch of Unthank Road between present day Grosvenor and Clarendon Roads, with part of the estate extending rearwards, down the steep hill as far as Mill Hill Road (which does not appear on the 1842 tithe map). But by the time of the first Norwich OS map in the 1880s the estate was only partly developed. Forming three sides of a rectangle around the estate (with Unthank Road forming the fourth side) was Grove Street West, Grove Street North and Grove Street East – the names of the streets reflecting their location in Heigham Grove. Eventually, these would become Grosvenor Road, Bathurst Road, and Clarendon Road. Bathurst Road was named for Henry Bathurst, Bishop of Norwich, who had died the same year as William Unthank, 1837.

37. PLAQUE ON BOARDMAN'S OFFICES

Philip Haldinstein owned a shoe factory in the city centre that, until the 1960s, occupied most of the land between Princes Street and Queen Street[24]. This was just a few yards away from Edward Boardman's own offices in Old Bank of England Court off Queen Street, where his name plaque can still be seen (fig 37). Just after the war Haldinstein's son George sold his 51% share to his partners, the Swiss firm Bally. Philip Haldinstein was a prominent Jewish businessman whose family burial plot can be seen in the Jewish part of Earlham Cemetery.

HEIGHAM GROVE ESTATE

Neville Street was once a cul-de-sac off Bathurst Road, denied access to Unthank Road by a parcel of land containing the house; this was labelled on the sale map 'Haldinstein'. The sale of Haldinstein's plot on Steward's estate allowed Neville Street – previously a short cul-de-sac – to join Unthank Road by extending the roadway between what were once Steward's buildings.

Before leaving the Steward estate it is worth noting that it is situated within Heigham Grove, as the temporary names of Grove Street acknowledged. Since 1973 this area has been recognised as the Heigham Grove Conservation Area [25], which occupies a ragged triangle formed by Park Lane, Earlham Road and Unthank Road. At about the time William Unthank moved out of the city into his Heigham estate, horse-drawn traffic coming into Norwich along Earlham Road would have travelled straight into the city via St Giles' Gate, demolished in 1794. But in the second half of the C20 even the footprint of the Gates would disappear beneath the Grapes' Hill segment of the ring road. Now, city-bound traffic along Earlham Road has to reflex back up Unthank Road, forming an uncomfortable fiddler's elbow. This mini-triangle within the Golden Triangle contains some of the most hilly parts of the city whose irregular street pattern and 'hidden' spaces were dictated by the occurrence of ancient chalk and flint mines [25]. The many large detached villas found here would have been built when the City Gaol occupied the apex of this area (1826-1890). Bryant's map of 1826 (fig 24) simply labels the site as 'New Jail' but Morant's map of 1873 (fig 23) shows the City Gaol to be an octagonal building in 'modern' radial form. Not many years later it was demolished to make way for St John the Baptist Catholic Cathedral and a new gaol was constructed on Mousehold Heath.

38. PLANTATION GARDEN FOUNTAIN MADE FROM GUNTONS' 'FANCY' BRICKS.

A notable feature of this area is the mid C19 Plantation Garden, situated in a former quarry probably made by mining flint (fig 38,39) [26]. It was designed by local furniture-maker Henry Trevor, whose own house was built nearby (fig 40). Architect Boardman is thought to have been involved in laying out the Plantation Garden as well as a fine seven-house terrace in adjacent Chester Place [27]. This 'secret' garden was constructed in Victorian Gothic style, with Italianate terraces, a fountain, and a palm house that has not survived. On Edward Boardman's sale map of the Eaton Lodge Estate (fig 27), based on Steward's land, Trevor is shown as a purchaser of a plot running from Unthank Road along the north side of present day Clarendon Road. Indeed, his sale of this land in 1897, 20 years after purchase, allowed the fuller development of Clarendon Road [27]. Trevor's family owned several plots in this area for in addition to his own land around Chester Place, his father-in-law owned The Grove and his stepson owned The Elms.

In the Plantation Garden the elaborate fountain, walkways and retaining walls are constructed from red or white 'fancy' bricks [28]. These were obtained, possibly as seconds, from Guntons' Brick Yard at Costessey. Guntons' Tudorbethan chimneys, tiles and letter bricks provided much to the texture of Victorian Norwich. In Heigham Grove they can be seen: on the gable end of Earlham Road terrace at the junction of Earlham Road with Belvoir Street (1853); on Adelaide Villa, Park Lane (1861); and on Aucuba Villas (fig 41) just down the hill from the Plantation Garden (1896).

39. THE PLANTATION GARDEN 1992. © georgeplunkett.co.uk

40. HENRY TREVOR'S HOUSE (BUILT 1856) IN 1992. ©georgeplunkett.co.uk

41. 'AUCUBA VILLAS' IN GUNTONS LETTER BRICKS, EARLHAM ROAD.

CHURCHES AND CHAPELS

Until the suburbanisation of South Heigham, St Bartholomew's (near present-day Waterworks Road) was the parish church for a largely dispersed and rural population. It was where William Unthank worshipped and where he was buried. In 1942 the church was to be bombed in a Baedeker Raid and the congregation forced to make use of the empty Primitive Methodist church in nearby Nelson Street [29]. Only the tower of St Bartholomew's survives and stands in a park off St Bartholomew's Close (fig 7). However, following the creeping campaign of terraced-house building, created largely by the development of Unthank land, the medieval – and now rather distant – parish church was too small to cater for the rising population. As a result, four new parishes were created within Heigham: St Barnabas' church can still be seen at the corner of Heigham and Northumberland Streets; St Philip's church was built opposite the junction between Stafford Street and Heigham Road; and St Thomas' church was built on the west side of Earlham Road. Within the Golden Triangle itself, Holy Trinity (fig 42) was erected in 1860 between Trinity and Essex Streets on land that CWJ Unthank, in a letter to the Eastern Daily Press, said had been donated by his father [4] (although Rosemary O'Donoghue states was sold to the Ecclesiastical Commissioners for £800 [19]). Certainly, this fine Gothic Revival, flint-clad church arose in the first phase of building on the Unthank estate, some years before the terraces would encroach upon Unthank's House further down the road. Another fine neo-Gothic, flint church – Christchurch – was built in the 1870s just off Christchurch Road. This was in the neighbouring parish of Eaton, which occupies the southern half of the Triangle, and would have catered for worshippers from the large detached villas in that part of the Triangle.

Non-conformist places of worship had been tolerated since the reign of Elizabeth I and the Old Meeting House and The Octagon Chapel in Colegate are famous early examples of separatist churches within the confines of the city walls. Within the Triangle, Edward Boardman built a Methodist

42. HOLY TRINITY CHURCH, TRINITY STREET.

chapel in Gothic style (1874), just outside St Giles' Gate at the city end of Unthank Road [29]. It was not to survive 100 years and in 1954 it was demolished to make way for the modernist Trinity United Reformed Church that stands today (fig 43). This was designed for Boardman and Son by a former member of the practice who came to national fame – Sir Bernard Melchior Feilden – who was responsible for supervising the completion of the new University of East Anglia after their split with Sir Denys Lasdun. The new church on Unthank Road represented an amalgamation of denominations and in recognition of this the original foundation stone from the Presbyterian church on Theatre

43. TRINITY UNITED REFORMED CHURCH, UNTHANK ROAD.

Street (which had been bombed in 1942) can be seen at the Unthank Road site. The modernist design of the church is often said to be influenced by Swedish mid-century style [e.g. 27] although Feilden himself said it was based on a church near Ravenna, Italy [30].

One of the more interesting small places of worship is the Swedenborgian Chapel Park Lane. It was designed in Victorian Gothic style by Augustus Scott ca 1890 and funded by an editor of the Eastern Daily Press who lived in Park Lane. Swedenborgianism was based on the beliefs of a C18 Swedish philosopher, Emanuel Swedenborg, who received millennialist revelations about the second coming of Christ. The chapel is now used for meetings and concerts [31].

Not far away, at the junction of Park Lane and Avenue Road, is St Peter's Park Lane [29]. This large chapel, built in 1939 to a design by Edward Boardman and Son, replaced the Wesleyan Methodist chapel (1894) that once stood on this prominent crossroads. At the time of writing it stands locked and the porch buttressed with heavy timber supports. Near the church at the corner of Unthank Road and Park Lane was The Elms, which contained the almshouses and staff social club for Mackintosh's chocolate

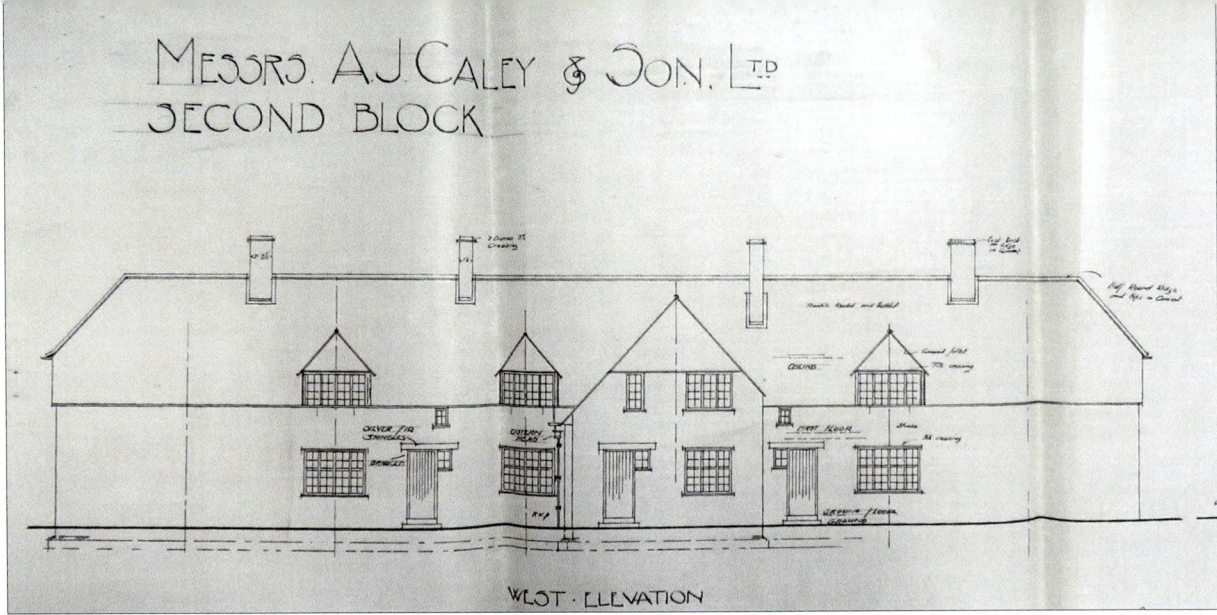

44. GEORGE SKIPPER'S PLANS FOR ALMSHOUSES AT THE ELMS. Courtesy NRO N/EN 24/150.

factory (originally Caley's) in Chapelfield. Lord Mackintosh worshipped in St Peter's. In 1956 he had been put in charge of introducing Premium Bonds; however, the minister objected to this form of gambling and organised a petition. Shaking his hand after Sunday service, Mackintosh gave the minister a wry smile and said, "I'm sorry that I won't be able to sign your petition" [32].

St Peter's is a large church but the Chapelfield Road Methodist Church, just inside the Triangle on the inner ring road opposite Chapelfield shopping mall, is larger and was built to accommodate 1000 worshippers. The most imposing place of worship, though, is undoubtedly the Catholic Cathedral of St John the Baptist, which overlooks the city from its vantage point at the junction of Unthank and Earlham Roads (fig 45). The Duke of Norfolk commissioned George Gilbert Scott to design the building. It was begun in 1884 and took the next 26 years to complete. Scott, however, died in 1897 and the work was completed by his brother John Oldrid Scott [27]. Considering the date it may be surprising that – apart from the interior furnishings and the stained glass – the church shows little contemporary style but it was the duke himself who had insisted on the purity of lancet-windowed Early English. The church became a cathedral in 1976.

Opposite the cathedral, on the opposite side of Earlham Road, is the Norwich Hebrew Congregation Synagogue, built in 1968. The original mid-C19 synagogue in Synagogue Street (the only street in the country with such a name), which was on the other opposite bank of the river from the present-day Riverside complex, was bombed in the 1942 air raids [29].

> With his eyes fixed to the skies as he left the chapel, Lord Mackintosh – who in 1932 had taken over Caley's chocolate factory – could have just seen the tops of the almshouses at The Elms that had been built around the sports and social club for his employees. This site at the corner of Park Lane and Unthank Road had been that part of Timothy Steward's estate labelled 'Shrubbery' on the 1842 tithe map. Under Caley's ownership, the architect and surveyor George Skipper drew designs (1919-1920) for an additional two blocks of cottages in Arts and Crafts style, arranged around the bowling green and tennis court (fig 44).

45. THE CATHOLIC CATHEDRAL OF ST JOHN THE BAPTIST.

THE EATON HALF OF THE GOLDEN TRIANGLE

The northern boundary of the parish of Eaton bisects the Golden Triangle just north of Mount Pleasant. The southern part of the Golden Triangle was therefore largely under the jurisdiction of Eaton parish rather than Heigham and was built on land owned by the Dean and Chapter of Norwich Cathedral. We have seen that the 1842 tithe map of Heigham (fig 32) placed the bulk of Unthank land in that parish but the 1838/9 Eaton tithe map (fig 46) shows that the parish boundary placed some of the estate known as 'Unthank's House' in Eaton; church tithes therefore had to be paid to two parishes. In addition to the southern edge of Clement William's estate within Eaton, he also owned a six acre plot on the west side of Unthank Road, abutting the large ecclesiastical estate to the south. This western part of the family's land would give rise to Warwick, Dover, Portland and Lincoln Streets – all running perpendicularly off Unthank Road with Portersfield Road to the rear. Leading away from the city the next side streets are College Road and Glebe Road but these were now on church land ('glebe' being the land that traditionally supported the parish priest). The first edition of the Ordnance Survey map shows that development of this western side of Unthank Road had hardly begun by the mid 1880s and, as we will see, when development came it was to be piecemeal.

Fifty years after this tithe map was made, George Skipper was to draw up a proposal on behalf of the Ecclesiastical Commissioners for roads in 'Eaton Glebe and South Heigham' [33]. Skipper designed some of the architectural 'fireworks' in the city centre (e.g. Norwich Union's Marble Hall, the Royal Arcade, Norfolk Daily Standard offices [34]) but he evidently took on the humbler aspects of an architect's life for in 1892 he sent a map and letter to the City Engineer concerning sewerage. This related to a road "to be called Recreation Road" ... "the houses being of less rental than £16 per annum"[33]. At this time Skipper's office was still in Opie Street where, in 1891, he was employing about 50 people.

46. EATON 1839 TITHE MAP. A SMALL PART OF THE UNTHANK ESTATE (PINK STAR) WAS IN EATON, AS WAS A SIX-ACRE PLOT (BLUE STAR) ON THE OTHER SIDE OF UNTHANK ROAD (YELLOW LINE). MOUNT PLEASANT (RED LINE).
NRO BR276/1/0798. Open Government Licence

In 1896 Skipper moved to 7 London Street where – although architects were not supposed to advertise – he displayed his skills on the decorative terracotta plaques outside his new offices, now subsumed into Jarrolds Department Store. One of the terracotta panels shows Skipper – with some of his large Norwich projects in the background – presenting a carved shield to clients (fig 47). The figure holding the shield resembles James Minns, a local 'carver' – a sculptor who did work for Guntons Brickyard in Costessey [28].

Skipper also designed several ornate neo-Georgian houses on College Road (fig 48) [35]. They have projecting rusticated door surrounds topped by a broken pediment, illustrating a distinct departure from the no-frills frontages of the Unthank terraces. Another major point of difference to the early Unthank house is the predominance on the Eaton Glebe estate of "good red kiln bricks" as specified in

47. GEORGE SKIPPER ADVERTISING HIS SKILLS. PLAQUE OUTSIDE JARROLDS DEPARTMENT STORE.

the restrictive covenants. The different texture of College Road can also be attributed to the different restrictions governing the adornment of the frontages. This long and architecturally variable street is distinguished in places by projections from the front elevation. The timber additions to the Arts and Crafts frontages on the first 100 yards or so off Unthank Road provide a great decorative impact – one that would not have found favour on early Unthank houses. While houses on the Unthank estate look back to Georgian plainness and uniformity the sporadic eruption of door canopies, bay windows and roof dormers along College Road reveal an ownership free to celebrate high Victorian style. Rosemary O'Donoghue [19] has traced this difference to the fact that the covenants on Eaton Glebe allowed owners to retain a degree of control over future developments. On this estate the plans for prospective houses had to be approved by every purchaser and this, combined with the fact that individual architects were generally only responsible for small blocks of houses, ensured that College Road is such a gloriously varied street.

48. SKIPPER HOUSES ON COLLEGE ROAD

49. FORMER TRAINING COLLEGE, COLLEGE ROAD. Edwardian postcard, author's collection.

College Road was named for the 'Norwich and Ely Training College for Schoolmistresses' that moved to new premises on this street (fig 49) from the old college on St George's Plain [36]. Opened in 1892 it was bombed 50 years later during the Baedeker air raids and moved to Keswick Hall on the outskirts of the city. The college had been situated in the centre of a block between The Avenues and Earlham Road and between College and Recreation Roads, on the site of the present-day Parkside School; this was near to Avenue Road Board School that had just opened.

On the opposite side of Recreation Road to the training college was the recreation field for which the road is named. The 1905-8 OS map shows that the ground was in existence before the houses had encroached from the Unthank Road end. In fact, the street plan for much of the Ecclesiastical Commissioners' land was still to be built upon. A plan drawn up by George Skipper in 1910 (now at his London Street offices) shows his proposed 'building sites' around four sides of the playing field that was to become Heigham Park (fig 50); the map is also interesting for labelling the adjacent Recreation Ground with the initials C.E.Y.M.S [37].

The initials CEYMS stand for Church of England Young Men's Society whose football team, known locally as 'Churches', won the Suffolk and Norfolk League ahead of the team that had broken away from them – Norwich City [38]. How many children – or even parents – at Recreation Road Infant School know that their playing fields may well have rung to 'On the Ball, City', The Canaries' football chant that is suggested to have been borrowed from CEYMS?

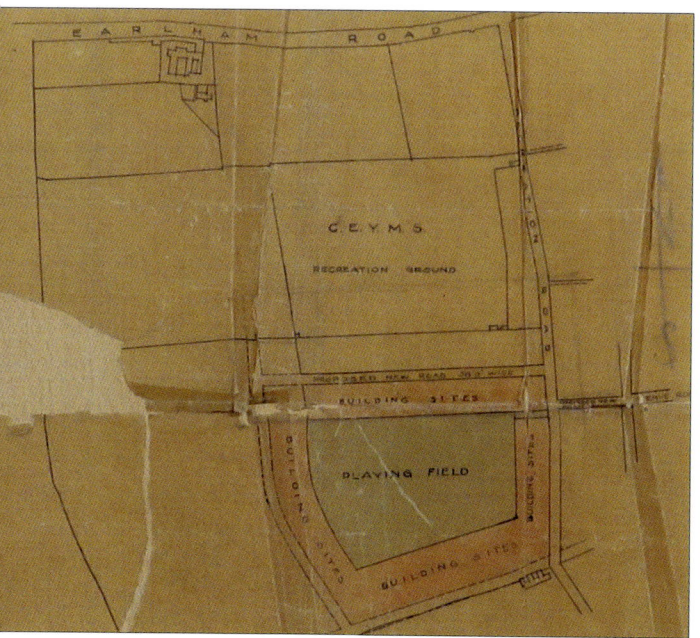

50. GEORGE SKIPPER'S ORIGINAL PLAN FOR HEIGHAM PARK.
Courtesy NRO N/EN 24/138.

HEIGHAM PARK

At one time the Recreation Ground adjoined a larger area known as Heigham Playing Fields. The Norwich Playing Fields and Open Spaces Society had purchased the land so that children in council schools – Crooks Place School (now Bignold) and Avenue Road Schools – could enjoy sports and recreation [39, 40]. The playing fields were opened in 1909. But by the 1920s the suburbanisation of South Heigham had crept as far as this open ground; some was offered for building while ca 2.5 hectares was carved out to form Heigham Park. George Skipper's plan (fig 50) for the reduced playing field was to build houses around all four sides with the upper side lying along what is now The Avenues. Fortunately, this fourth row of houses was not built and as a consequence The Avenues continues without deviation as it merges into Avenue Road.

Heigham Park is very much a twentieth century creation. After the First World War a former soldier, Captain Arnold Edward Sandys-Winsch, was appointed by the council as 'Parks and Allotments Superintendent of Norwich City Parks Department' [40]. He was eventually to draw up plans for Heigham Park as well as Wensum, Eaton and Waterloo Parks and Mile Cross Gardens. Much of the work was funded by national work-creation schemes designed to support unemployed returning soldiers. As open expansive areas, these parks provided a counterpoint to densely inhabited areas of the medieval city. Heigham was started first, it took three years to build and was opened in 1924. It was the smallest of the Sandys-Winsch parks and although it didn't have the buildings that characterise Eaton and Waterloo Parks it did have tennis courts, bowling greens and rock gardens. Sandys-Winsch had trained under the renowned landscape architect Thomas Mawson who had taught him to draw up excellent plans and to appreciate the importance of trees as can be seen in the tree-lined walkways at Heigham Park, The Avenues and nearby Eaton Park. Sandys-Winsch also left a larger legacy to the city and to the Golden Triangle in particular. These were the avenues

51. GOBLET-PRUNED AMERICAN PLANE TREES ON EARLHAM ROAD.

52. SUNFLOWER GATES AT HEIGHAM PARK.

of American plane trees pruned into goblet shapes that characterise Earlham Road as well as the Triangle's lower boundary along the A140 ring road/Colman Road (fig 51). Trees are such an important part of an enlightened urban streetscape and we must thank Captain Sandys-Winsch for having planted an estimated 20,000.

The entrance to Heigham Park is marked by iron gates in the form of sunflowers (fig 52). These are modern reproductions of the sunflower railings that once stood around an ornate iron pagoda in Chapelfield Gardens from 1880 until its postwar destruction (visit [41] for a fuller account). The pagoda was demolished in 1949 and some of these original sunflower railings were re-used as gates to the tennis courts. The ornate two-storey pagoda – which became emblematic of the late C19 Aesthetic Movement that celebrated Japanese design – was conceived by Wymondham architect Thomas Jeckyll, and made by the Norfolk Ironworks of Barnard Bishop and Barnards in Coslany.

THE PARK TOWN ESTATE

We have already encountered this estate on the northwest side of Avenue Road when it belonged to the private asylum called The Retreat. Street plans made by surveyors Wright and Ratcliffe in 1886, [42] not shown) record interesting differences from the current road names. It was proposed that Caernarvon Road, which had already advanced up the hill from Earlham Road, should connect directly with Avenue Road via an extension named Bangor Road. However, the construction of Avenue Road Board School intervened to block that connection. Regulations stipulated that all these Welsh-named roads on the estate should be 30 feet wide. Avenue Road itself was a generous 36 feet wide, for which modern-day drivers can breathe a sigh of relief after threading the needle of the surrounding car-lined streets. Until 1893 Pembroke Road was called Garden Road – implying the location of garden ground – and explains the naming of The Garden House pub (1879) at the junction with Denbigh Road. It is interesting to see that the eponymous avenue of trees was still marked on the map, from the junction of Avenue Road with Park Lane as far as Garden Road.

THE AVENUE ESTATE

A plan dated 1898 shows the roads and services for 'Mrs C Porter's Estate. Proposed new streets from College Road to Park Lane Norwich' (fig 53, [43]). Evidently Mrs Porter's estate stretched from that part of Avenue Road between the school and Park Lane together with Whitehall Road and the west side of Portersfield Road (presumably named for Porter's field). The plan also shows a road from Warwick Street into the back of Rose Valley that never materialised, leaving it a cul-de-sac.

The various maps and plans of Heigham and Eaton over the second half of the C19 underline the slow, uneven development of the Triangle. Land owners employed architects and surveyors to lay out their individual building plots and this piecemeal approach was to continue well in the C20. For instance George Skipper was seeking permission to extend The Avenues to Jessopp Road as late as 1926 [44]. Although plans had to be approved by the City Engineer it is hard to shake off the impression that instead of slotting into an overarching design the estates' architects were trying to force-fit their own piece of the jigsaw puzzle.

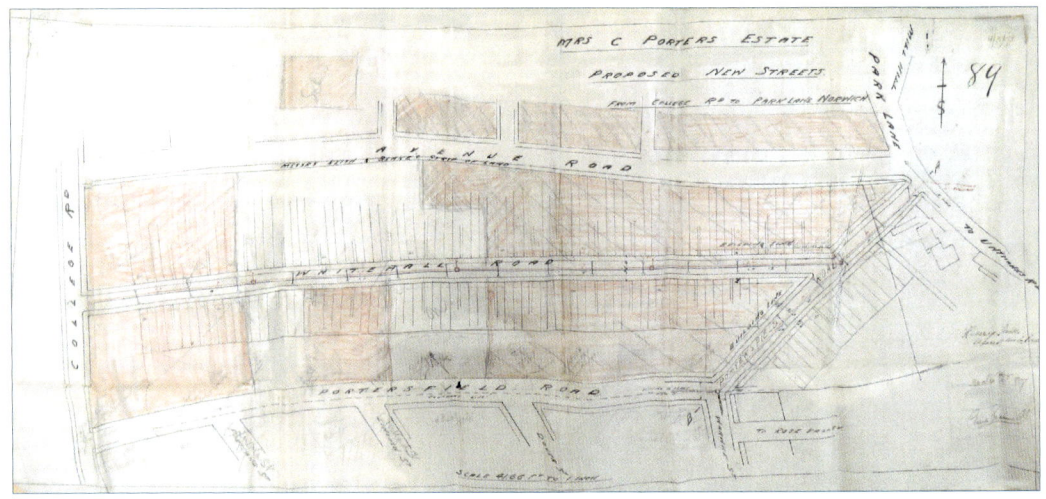

53. MRS PORTER'S ESTATE. Courtesy of Norfolk Record Office N/EN 24/89

This ad hoccery is illustrated by a letter written in 1930 to the City Engineer from the Avenue Road Council School concerning building developments on the site between Whitehall and Portersfield Roads [45]. The Secretary for Education wrote that if the whole site were to be developed there would be no direct access to the school from Portersfield Road, Warwick, Dover and other streets, requesting – rather plaintively – for at least a passageway to be kept open.

THE SOUTHWESTERN TRIANGLE

Throughout the early C20 George Skipper was an important figure in the development of the southern part of the Triangle below College Road. In 1914 he submitted a plan for a new road, 'College Road to Eaton Park' [46] (not shown). This is now Jessopp Road and extends from Portersfield Road down to Colman Road, part of the present-day ring road. It is interesting to see that although Highland, Muriel and Mornington Roads – which run parallel to Unthank Road – are already indicated on this map, the next block consisted of allotment gardens (now the Meadow Rise estate). As a consequence, Christchurch Road was arrested at the junction with Highland Road. The completion of Christchurch Road from Unthank Road through to Earlham Road was to wait another twenty years before Skipper laid out this extension, well after the Corporation had adopted The Avenues and Jessopp Road.

In a letter dated 1st March 1934, proposing this new road [47] (fig 54), the Ecclesiastical Commissioners expressed puzzlement as to why the council had not already used public funds to push Christchurch Road through to Earlham Road. They carefully outlined the ownership of land alongside the proposed road. For example, between The Avenues and Earlham Road was a playing field belonging to the Girls Public Day School Trust who, the

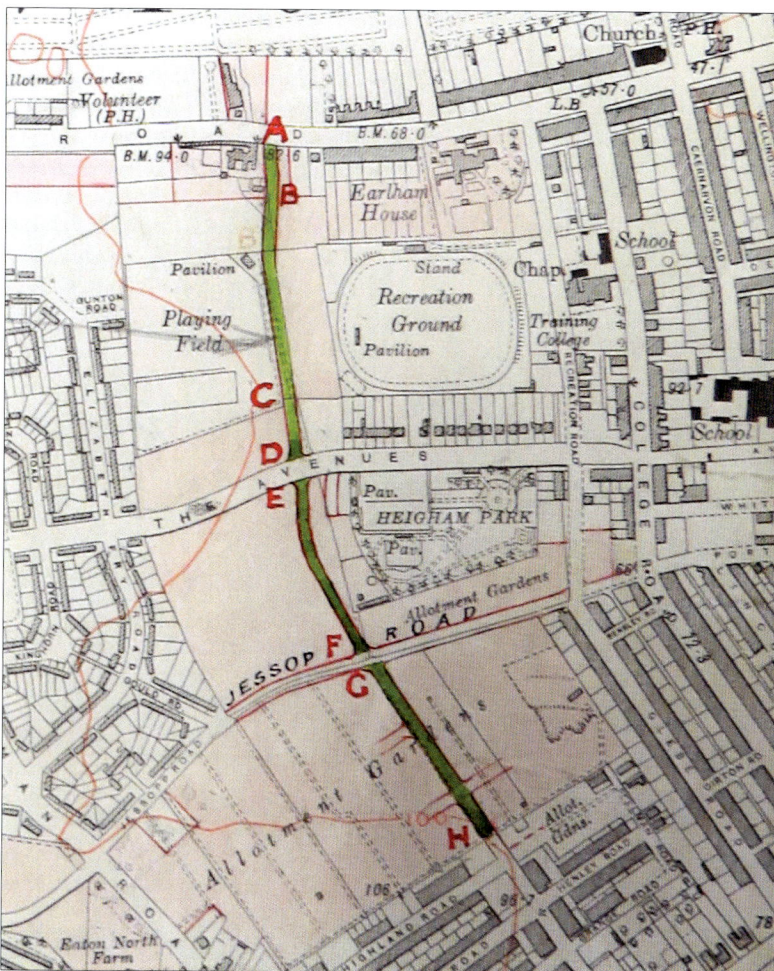

54. PROPOSED CHRISTCHURCH ROAD EXTENSION TO EARLHAM ROAD.
Courtesy Norfolk Record Office CHC addl/S/1/3 Map © Ordnance Survey.

Commissioners calculated, would be liable to pay £750 towards the road. The letter was evidently effective for a week later the Commissioners authorised "the payment not exceeding £20,100 in constructing the roads." George Skipper was responsible for laying out the road and drains,

55. CHRISTCHURCH ROAD LEADING TO EARLHAM ROAD CA 1935. Courtesy NRO CHC addl/S/1/3

sub-contracting the roadworks to Edward J Edwards. The works progressed across the Highland Road allotments for which several allotment holders required compensation from the Ecclesiastical Commissioners – a Mr Wilson requiring compensation for the loss of his field of 'Mangolds' (mangelwurzels used for stockfeed) [47]. A photograph (ca 1935) in the Norfolk Record Office [47] (fig 55) shows the completion of Christchurch Road as it joined Earlham Road. As the caption to a similar photo in the local newspaper, The Journal, stated, "thus providing through communication from the latter road to Ipswich Road". This implies that the Ecclesiastical Commissioners' intention was to provide an east-west shortcut between Ipswich and Earlham Roads. However, by then the parallel stretch of the modern-day ring road (Colman Road) had already been built, so rather than providing a duplicate shortcut it is more likely that the commissioners were more driven to open up their estate.

On this part of the ring road, at the junction of Coleman Road with The Avenues, the council built the Earlham branch library in 1929 (fig 56). Above its entrance is a Classical open pediment with attractive Arts and Crafts calligraphy. A similarly styled Mile Cross branch library was to be built in 1931 on Aylsham Road, on the opposite side of the city.

56. EARLHAM BRANCH LIBRARY

THE EATON GROVE ESTATE

Before Christ Church Eaton was built, the eastern end of Christchurch Road between Unthank and Newmarket Roads was known as Eaton Grove Road. This road ran parallel to what would become the ring road/Mile End Road and, between these two roads, three large plots were marked on the 1838 Eaton tithe map as 'Inclosures' belonging to Horatio Bolingbroke who was JP, Mayor and first Sheriff of Norwich. Later, Christ Church Eaton was to be built on a circular plot in the centre of this estate, with access from Mile End and Eaton Grove Roads. In the last quarter of the C19 surveyor Charles Horner subdivided the entire area into 20 plots for sale by 'Messrs Butcher'.[48] (fig 57).

Bolingbroke & Co were involved in the city's wine trade, owning the Wine Vault in Upper St Giles Street and, in 1886, the Norwich Wine Company[49]. Throughout the C19, various members of the Bolingbroke family owned land in the Christchurch Road area, including Sir John Harrison Yallop (mayor 1815, 1831) who is interred in the Bolingbroke family vault in the churchyard of St Peter Mancroft. Yallop was a goldsmith and his brother-in-law Nathaniel Bolingbroke (founder of the Norwich branch of Bolingbrokes[50]) was a silversmith.

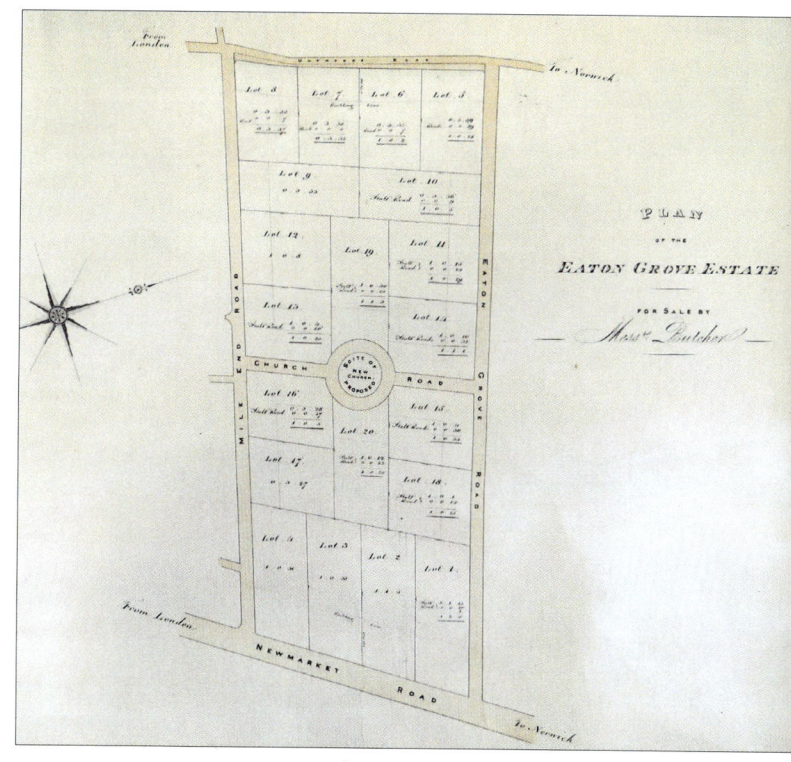

57. EATON GROVE ESTATE. Courtesy NRO BR276/1/0622

NEWMARKET ROAD

The Eaton tithe map marks the ownership of land between Eaton Grove/Christchurch Road and the Unthank estate to the north [51]. At that time there were fewer than 20 buildings in this part of Eaton – all non-terraced and some substantial. On the north side of the junction of Christchurch and Newmarket Road, Horatio Bolingbroke owned, but did not occupy, a large estate labelled 'mansion and pleasure grounds'. This mansion – now owned by the Norwich High School for Girls (fig 58) – was where Sir Charles Gilman was to move after he departed from Unthanks House in Heigham, just a few hundred yards away.

Large Victorian properties were built further along Newmarket Road, one of the most attractive being the Regency-styled terrace (numbers 47 to 69) with the middle four bays projecting under a pediment [27] (fig 59). The terrace was built between William Unthank's estate and the Eaton to Norwich Road (Newmarket Road). As the deeds to number 47 record, it was built on farmland leased in 1825 from the Bishop of Norwich, illustrating the reach of the Bishopric Estate on this side of the city. In 1828/1829 the builder Edward Browne erected this row of 12 houses – then called St Stephen's Terrace – screened from the road by jointly-owned pleasure grounds.

This unified terrace, with its central pediment and doorways dressed with fluted columns, offers a richer version of the Georgian classical ideal than the plainer Unthank terraces to be built in the decades to come. However, Georgian gentility came at a cost and half a century later it was to give way to the need to house the large numbers of workers who were coming off the land to support the city's thriving industries and businesses. Modern-day occupants can give thanks to the quality of the Golden Triangle's buildings (and the planning laws) that ensured these terraces continue to provide comfortable housing into the twenty-first century.

58. NORWICH HIGH SCHOOL FOR GIRLS
Courtesy Norwich High School for Girls

59. ST STEPHEN'S TERRACE, NEWMARKET ROAD.

ACKNOWLEDGEMENTS

This account of the Golden Triangle has been greatly enhanced by the photographs of the Unthanks. I am therefore deeply grateful to Richard Gordon, Lord of Intwood, for allowing me to reproduce the Unthank family photographs; Julian Darling for permission to reproduce the Besche portrait of CWJ Unthank and James Darling for photographing the portrait; Andrea Spooner of Fosters Solicitors and Michael Mcaully of designcompany.co.uk for providing the portrait of William Unthank. I also thank David Clark of the City Bookshop for background on the Unthanks in Heigham; Rosemary O'Donoghue for discussions on Unthank's House; John Litster for suggesting I expand my blog posts on the Unthanks into a small book on the Golden Triangle; Alastair Grieve for information on St Stephen's Crescent; to Jonathan Plunkett for access to his father's wonderful collection of photographs; the staff of the Norfolk Record Office and of the Heritage Centre in Norwich Millennium Library for cheerfully helping me with my many requests. I am indebted to my friend the designer Karen Roseberry for transforming my writing into the finished article.

REFERENCES

1. Ordnance Survey TG20; surveyed 1938-1952: 1956. Courtesy National Library of Scotland
2. Heigham 1842 tithe map NRO BR276/1/0051. A clearer version made for Holy Trinity is PD 522/44. Open Government Licence.
3. Trudgill, Peter (2016). Dialect Matters: Respecting Vernacular Language. Pub: Cambridge University Press.
4. Letter from Colonel CWJ Unthank, Eastern Daily Press, Letters, May 25 1934.
5. Rye, Walter (1917). History of the Parish of Heigham in the City of Norwich. Pub: Roberts & Co Ten Bells Lane but available online http://welbank.net/norwich/hist.html
6. A History of Fosters Solicitors http://www.fosters-solicitors.co.uk/downloads/fosters-history.pdf
7. Nixseaman, A.J. (1972). The Intwood Story (private imprint).
8. Norfolk Record Office NRS 4150
9. NRO MC 279/6. Letter, Miss M Nicols of Dawlish
10. NRO MC279/17/1-8, 697x2. papers of Heigham Hall private mental hospital.
11. https://www.psychologytoday.com/blog/lunacy-and-mad-doctors/201505/did-the-victorian-asylum-allow-the-rich-evade-justice
12. NRO DS240
13. NRO MC 191/2
14. NRO N/CCH83-90 (see N/MC Trustees of Municipal Charities)
15. NRO N/TC/D1/277, 335x2
16. NRO CHC 170770. Heigham-next-Norwich manor court books, volume 'F'. Eaton, volume 'E'.
17. Bell's Weekly Messenger Sunday 19 November 1837. From the British Newspaper Archive.
18. NRO DN/TA723
19. O'Donoghue, Rosemary (2014). Norwich, an Expanding City 1801-1900. Pub: The Larks Press
20. NRO MC1319/1-22
21. Muthesius, Stefan (1984). The English Terraced House. Pub: Yale University Press.

22. http://freepages.genealogy.rootsweb.ancestry.com/~haslatter/history/bowdens/bk/f4730.htm#source
23. MC 191/2
24. https://colonelunthanksnorwich.com/2016/07/28/norwichs-pre-loved-buildings/
25. https://www.norwich.gov.uk/downloads/file/3010/heigham_grove_conservation_area_appraisal
26. http://plantationgarden.co.uk/
27. Pevsner, Nikolaus and Wilson, Bill (2002). The Buildings of England. Norfolk I: Norwich and North-East. Pub: Yale University Press.
28. https://colonelunthanksnorwich.com/2016/05/05/fancy
29. https://colonelunthanksnorwich.com/2017/08/15/post-medieval-norwich-churches/
30. https://historicengland.org.uk/listing/the-list/list-entry/1392268
31. http://www.norfolkchurches.co.uk/norwichsweden/norwichsweden.htm
32. http://www.norfolkchurches.co.uk/norwichparklanemeth/norwichparklanemeth.htm
33. NRO N/EN 24/34
34. https://colonelunthanksnorwich.com/2017/02/15/the-flamboyant-mr-skipper/
35. NRO N/EN 12/1/2190
36. http://keswickhallcollege.schools.uk.com/
37. NRO N/EN 24/138
38. https://en.wikipedia.org/wiki/Norwich_CEYMS_F.C.
39. https://historicengland.org.uk/listing/the-list/list-entry/1001347
40. Anderson, A.P. and Cocke, S. (2000). The Captain and the Norwich Parks. Pub: The Norwich Society.
41. https://colonelunthanksnorwich.com/2016/01/06/jeckyll-and-the-sunflower-motif/
42. NRO N/EN 24/6
43. NRO N/EN 24/89
44. NRO N/EN/164
45. NRO N/EN 24/89
46. NRO E/EN 24/147
47. NRO CHC addl/S/1/3
48. NRO BR 276/1/0622
49. norridge.me.uk/pubs/names_/firms/boling.htm
50. http://discovery.nationalarchives.gov.uk/details/r/785b3044-df6b-4c0b-acf8-658243 1efb6a
51. NRO BR276/1/0798

Unless otherwise stated all photographs are © 2017 Clive Lloyd.

BACK COVER: UNTHANK FAMILY CREST AT INTWOOD HALL. Courtesy of Richard Gordon.

FRONT COVER: PHOTO OF COLONEL CWJ UNTHANK Courtesy Richard Gordon; map ©Ordnance Survey